LATTER DAYS OF EVE

LATTER DAYS OF EVE

Beverly Burch

Winner of the John Ciardi Prize for Poetry
Selected by Patricia Spears Jones

BkMk Press
University of Missouri-Kansas City

BkMk Press
University of Missouri-Kansas City
5101 Rockhill Road
Kansas City, MO 64110

Executive Editor: Robert Stewart
Managing Editor: Ben Furnish
Assistant Managing Editor: Cynthia Beard

**Missouri
Arts Council**
The State of the Arts

Financial assistance for this book has been provided by the Missouri Arts Council, a state agency.

Cover art: Carol Jenkins (www.caroljenkinsart.com)
Author photo: Ellie Waxman

The John Ciardi Prize for Poetry wishes to thank Susan Cobin, Greg Field, Lindsey Martin-Bowen, Michael Nelson, Linda Rodriguez, and Maryfrances Wagner.

BkMk Press wishes to thank Rhiannon Minster and Michael Nelson.

Library of Congress Cataloging-in-Publication Data

Names: Burch, Beverly, author.
Title: Latter days of eve : poems / Beverly Burch.
Description: Kansas City, MO : BkMk Press/University of Missouri-Kansas
    City, [2019] | "Winner of the John Ciardi Prize for Poetry selected by
    Patricia Spears Jones." | Summary: "Latter Days of Eve imagines Eve's
    life after Eden, moving this and other biblical figures' ancient conflicts
    into contemporary settings in the Middle East, North America, and
    elsewhere"– Provided by publisher.
Identifiers: LCCN 2019024626 | ISBN 9781943491209 (paperback)
Classification: LCC PS3602.U7295 A6 2019 | DDC 811/.6–dc23
LC record available at https://lccn.loc.gov/2019024626

ISBN: 978-1-943491-20-9

This book is set in ITC Franklin Gothic and Peignot.

Contents

FOUR

FIVE

SIX

Latter Days of Eve

Congregation

This one shall be called Woman.
—Genesis 2:23

In the beginning I was the only one.
I questioned everything. No one answered.
This is what it means to be Woman.
A crazy aunt. Dangerous as a blue norther.
I fled from myself, walked into the Danakil,
hid in uncut coverts of boreal forest. Sped south
on an unmarked highway. In the great nowhere
I heard another woman weep, watched one
spew buckshot to the purple distance,
heard muttered incantations.
Many colors of flesh, languages crackling,
yet one called another. I drew closer.
One made a fire, one brought
a copper pot. Under a baobab a woman
sang like a child when no one listens. Cold
as a prehistoric shiver, no idea what might be next—
for the first time, I was not alone.

ONE

First Day Out of Eden

So much water. Translucence.
Billows and caverns. Eve paces
shoreline, nowhere further to flee.

In the blue swells a man's body
thrashes—he tried to walk
its shifting surface?

She devours fistfuls of gulfweed,
gulps the stinging sea,
vomits behind a dune.

False gods out here, she's heard.
On the sand a coiled mollusk—
exile of sea or land?

The voices say she's speaking
in tongues. What's a tongue?
she asks. What's a hallelujah?

What's an empty grave?
Sky is a smoky orange disk.
In the city, clappers and bells,

towers ringing like a heart.
What's a heart? What does it mean
when a hand's offered?

Pavement. Loud rushing things.
Terror rises up, flees past
in the slipstream.
In the foothills, she glimpses
the long flocculent tail of a fox.
Then giant sequoia—furrowed bark.
Fruit beyond reach.

Ms. Exodus

The last arid mountain.
A dessicating wind in an alien valley. Collapse.

Eve's heart sprouts black lilies.
Rich loam, wild garden—she imagined these?

Above, crows. And swallows.
Fierce they are out here, frenzied

predators of what lives in the air.
On rocky marl she dreams

she finds the man again, leaves him again.
Tiny hairs creep across her face.

Ants. Spider, centipede, scorpion.
A hundred-year tortoise looks on with pity.

In its eyes, appetite.
They crawl together toward vegetation.

Distant anthems of assault rifles,
clatter of tanks, blue song of IEDs.

But above, so many swallows,
birds she loves for how they sling

through the air, cross without colliding.

Patriarch

Upon this rock I will build my church.
—Matthew 16:18

Fall, fail. Adam hauled his failure to the desert,
weighty as dolomite, pitted and opaque.

He posted warnings on its ugly slab: *high voltage,
do not touch.*

The Sun was new, as he was.
He raised knuckled hands, cocked his face

to heaven. It blinded him, bronzed him like a calf.
Otherwise he'd never have stumbled

up to his dumb mouth in dust. Like a hulking
angel he beat his arms and legs.

After many days he heard faint singing,
faint wings, felt himself pulled free.

The slab still towered. He crawled
to its shadow, rested in shade: a God

who sheltered, with no grinding brilliance.
He gathered stones, built a path, a monument.

Made his God a cathedral.

The Morning After

Eve followed the tremble of streams
          heavy with water, jeweled scat of elk
and cougar. Through foothills crooked paths

led to a ghostly meadow. No grotto or den.
          She sheltered in a thatch of leaves
under peeling red shanks of madrone.

Something woolly grazed her in lemony
          moonlight. Apparition. Stranger, fiend.
Another wilderness beast. Weathered flesh

and matted beard. A man on his knees
          asking forgiveness. Hands touched
her cheek. Gentle supplication.

Adam. Adam. How long since they fled
          in opposite directions? A month?
A year? Her body rolled like soft fruit

from the stem to his lips, his chest,
          new again. So feral, tender.
Did they do it like this in the garden?

When sun washed the tangle of their legs,
          warm as a furred pelt, they turned away.
Now birdsong and the man's low hum

as he built a fire, threaded a mourning dove
          on a spiked stalk. And something
mechanical droning in a faraway sky.

Night Watch

The world turns inside out
in sleepless hours of the night. Eve floats

at its watery center until her poor brainpan
slips off the three hundred-count raft,
bobbing and plunging.

Everyday objects ride on the far side, traitorous
as suspected. Flotsam washes over.

Come-hither images of the ineffable, memories
on autodial: fruited limbs, snake, flaming angels at a gate.

A totem pops to the surface—winter tree
stripped of leaves, an inverted ribcage.

Wail of siren, scent of skunk.
There's the world again, the outside and its routine
dangers. Her new familiars.

Beauty of night's freedoms, doors
to the labyrinth. But she has a return ticket
to tomorrow where she'll unpack

her bags, let rumpled belongings eddy off.
Oh, light. Genesis. Its fated offerings

waiting at the dock. Smell of toast, footsteps
on the kitchen floor. His.

The Lilith Wind

Adam wanted her to lie beneath him, but Lilith insisted he lie below her. When Lilith saw they would never agree, she uttered God's Name and flew into the air.
—The Alphabet of Ben Sira

Eve, *ma doublure, ma soeur.* I'm whistling in the branches—
    both good and evil—your name in it.
Of course snakes insinuate. Parched by lies, wriggling out
    like skin, they fork their tongues and lisp *dogma.*

You begged to be finished with innocence
    but the mind's a rusted gate. Does not spring open.
So a snake slithered up and you climbed the tree
    hand over hand like a child.

Do not repent tasting, only that it was brief:
    now your hands itch as you stroke
any brown trunk with a smattering of leaves.

Adam named *oak, pine, ash.*
    I chose *honey locust, witch hazel, pussy willow.*

God lifted his big paws, sculpted me.
    Same clay as Adam, two lonely mutts.
Then Adam went at it. I taught him
    slow touch. Lips, legs, the freakish heart beat.
Pleasure arrived in the dark until I shrieked
    God oh God and confounded him.

Mystery of the body—spate of blood every month,
    then it ends. I vomited grassy soup, my belly
a stupendous apple, ready to drop.
    Inside something kicked like a small rabbit: love fruit.

Sharp Tooth

The snake waits off to the side,
coiled.

Keep an eye on the snake.

It's proud of its beauty.
Red and black skin. Yellow diamonds.
Long sinuous neck.
Its lovely head is a soft arrow,
waiting to fly.

Evicted in its genesis, it's a wound,
raw and thumping.

Its truth venom, its venom truth.

It means to deliver you from error.
It hisses, itching to strike,
yet full of remorse.

The snake can't stop being a snake.

TWO

Eve Embedded

Eve the temptress that we must beware of in any woman.
—St Augustine

Even as you trust him he tries to rule you.
Even if and even though
you practice his religion he martyrs you.
Eventually he forces you and every judge says he can.

From the spoils of innocence
eventuates the tree of knowledge:
Adam's breed fears you, fears to be like you.

Even-tempered as you try to be
he thunders and reviles. Even as you speak of peace,
missiles fly.

Eve, Eve! Even everything?

Can no one say it? His breed is dangerous.
Even money on it. Ever-present danger.

Everest and evergreens and Everglades.
Even-toed ungulates, none and nowhere safe.

Your everlasting faith, even still.
Everblooming lotus, prayer at eventide,
evensong's choir and belief in ever-changing dogma,
entreating mercy to fall evenhanded.

Sons, lovers, fathers, brothers,
friends, neighbors. Who knows what rises
from everted hearts of men's fear?

The Patriarch's Gifts

She tossed the golden amulet he sent
in the alligator's swamp
and watched it sink. Six reptilian eyes

flickered with hope. She opened
the brass box of his letters and fed them
to the bone fire. Page by page, words

curled into blackened bits,
off to a chilly hereafter. On the table:
basket of red apples, bowl of bloodroot.

From him she wants neither
bitter nor sweet. The nature of his poison
tethers them, blisters their nerves,

and they both know its fortitude,
how it lasts beyond remembering,
disappears, then surges back

until she returns for more.

Sororitas

A husk was created for the brain, and . . . brought forth . . . Lilith.
—Zohar 1:19b

Remember. Lilith warned—
man and woman, a disaster of desire.
Coitus exposes everything.

Your irretrievable sister. He loved her
like a wildfire loves Wyoming.
She took him naked to her body, saw it all:
his fragile vanity and swagger.

How unafraid she was, telling him she
was his equal. Imagine his rage.
He banished her on the spot, a frenzy
of obliteration, lover and unborn child.

Like Athena, birthed by a god,
delivered from his ponderous head.
Just to enter this world
she cracked his greatness open.

Old Friend

Now the snake was more astute than all.
—Genesis 3:1

Psst! Garden girl. My apple wife.
I'm here, your familiar, on the cold stone.
Your twisted tongue-and-groove scandalman.

Look what I risk for you—
the man who says he loves you
would peel off my skin, wear it
around his waist with a brass buckle.
The Man. A pontifex. A pox on him.

Your marriage is snake-bit.
A lopsided wagon, a yoked-up mess.
I'm a coiled scoundrel with no ears
but I listen better than he does—
midnight fears, outlawed things
you mutter while you mend.

Listen, poppet, it's chilly on the floor.
Pretend we're back in the garden
and I'll sibilate in the perfect curve of your ear.
Move over. Let's marry up some heat.

Motherhood Chronicles

Mother on Fire

She couldn't bear the dawdling or the chatter,
    even the child's fragrant warmth,
his toothsome weight, his wriggling. Days
    staggered, a broken animal

down a sour alley at daybreak.
    She picked through LEGOs, the splayed soldiers.
Tossed puzzle pieces in the same bin
    as books smeared with purple jam, a single muddy

sandal, his beloved rainbow-hued
    rubber snake. Motherhood. Snapped shut,
airless. Later she couldn't remember
    where she went—red rock territory,

silent blowouts of desert. She returned
    when she knew there'd be another.
Shopped in the desolate flourescence of mini-malls,
    cooked vegetables they wouldn't eat.

She held on in the painted house, roasted
    her husband's meat. As they settled into sleep
she counted minutes. Took scraps
    of paper to the basement, wrote what

her mind wouldn't claim, set fire to it.
    Hot and flying, she went up in smoke.
Five a.m. she fluttered like ash to earth.
    Climbed stairs to make jelly sandwiches.

October Noir

Mid-autumn morning opens like a film: gray clouds
in a cold sky. Intrigue, moods, a double-cross.

A woman walks the edge of an urban lake,
its inky waters whipped by wind. Soot-black

coots scuttle the surface, mallards root nervously
in sandy murk. She paces herself

to return in time for her eight-year-old who sits
in an office across the street talking about nightmares,

fear of strangers, snakes. With a therapist.
At least that's what the woman hopes they talk about.

She close-focuses on a live-oak: tiny leaves glisten
from a burst of rain. The stagnant north end

sends up a sour odor. Beer bottles sunk in slime,
fast food cups, tattered wrappers like paper lilies—

everything fits the movie. Except herself—*nothing to kill
but time,* good line for a woman who spends days

with her engine idling until school lets out,
soccer practice ends, choir's done. Again, the lake—

the lake is where the body is, turning now
to black jelly—yes, the smell!

That cloth snagged on a withered bush:
man's handkerchief, undetermined smears.

Behind the rocks, an evening purse. Danger's still to come.
The frail Asian woman mumbling as she stoops

to feed gulls, she's a decoy. The young black guy whistling
on his way somewhere sweet, thin jeans hanging off

his backside—no idea he's walking into someone else's
bad business. Herself, she's safe. Audience.

Love Scrawl

The first child to breach this world, Cain.
Out the door he flies, a raptor, plumed
and clawed. No stroking the dark

fringe of his hair. His brother's a moon-gawker.
Runs into the street after dogs,
flails on his bicycle toward a blind corner.

Brakes squeal, adrenaline hits
kindling sticks of her heart and she blazes.
Upstairs Dorcas slams her door.

The girl who once hunted with bow and arrow
is gorgeous now, a cat grooming herself
out of reach. But Elisheba

restores innocence. Her pocket holds
a folded love scrawl in swollen script,
"*i*"s dotted with hearts,

to a girl named Judith. The girls'
tank tops fit her. How tenderly
she lifts the wash as if she'll find tiny tees,

cottons with a milky sweetness.
Yesterday from the aisle of canned peaches
a baby's cry pumped ecstasy into her cells.

Oh Eve, every Eve. Three-day fevers,
bloodied lips and blistered feet,
the broken bone. Daily wounds, smeared kisses

bind her. She knows each fingerbreadth
of their bodies, yet they know
little of her, how deep they're lodged.

How defenseless the vacant portals
of a mother's flesh. These creatures
from who knows where.

They sing in their rooms, disappear
after midnight. They've cross-stitched
her insides, silk and briars.

Daughter Chord

With his immortal horses He who has many names . . . caught
her up reluctant . . . and bare her away.
          —Homer, Hymn to Demeter II

If she calls you'll be ready,
willing to scorch field and forest for her.

An estate half-buried in the countryside,
dimly lit, dank air. Inside the great hall
that devil took her to be his queen.

His face dazzled her, all cheekbones,
pout, cold diamond eyes.

Next he showed his gems. Red
and luculent as pomegranate seeds.
You know she wanted to resist them.

On the edge of being released
something in her said, *Touch them*.

How could she know so many would fall?
Mothers, even as they pin wet laundry to the line,
listen for the thump and groan,

chariot down the boulevard,
the hoofbeats' clopping.

Invocation to Time/No Time

A blessing on the endurance of childhood,
each moment a life as a whole hour runs over

the horizon. Blessing on the hard rooms
of old age, a dull curtain drawn against the city,

every day a lengthy pull toward dressing.
Blessings on in-between years when you raise

children in a blur. Minute of the stroller
at the back door, wooden rabbit on wheels.

No time for last night's dishes, laundry sporing
on summer nights. A benediction for how soon

the house will be too quiet. For how only once
or twice time opens its latch and you step out,

catch stillness, silence of air. Mercy
and a curse that all time may be synchronous

yet the needle keeps flying through the cloth.

THREE

At the Longest Red Light

*The angels come to visit us, and we only know them when
they are gone.*

—George Eliot, Scenes of Clerical Life

A woman in a blue sedan
sweeps air with her hands,
exactly conducting the Dvořák on Eve's CD.

Windows up, the woman couldn't hear it
and, modest in her hijab, doesn't seem the type,
but she *adagios* her arms, raising violins.

Left, right, left, rows them to a slow fever,
fleet undulation of fingers calls in
clarinets. Oh, virtuosity in her hands.

Now flute. Palms forward, a flurry,
molto vivace, and a shift into the *allegro*.
The full O of the moon hangs over

three neon Os in the Whole Foods sign.
Light turns green, Eve races to keep up.
The woman *prestos.* Left hand strokes final chords

in closure. God, she loves this woman.
Who grips the wheel, turns to freeway.
Eve shivers, brakes. No one beside her now

but a BMW gunning to cut her off.

Pantoum That Can't Sleep

Thou shalt be as one sleeping in the midst of the sea.
—Proverbs 23:34

You have to enter sleep like water
without trying to swim.
It's a skill, slipping below the line,
vanishing into the unseen.

Without trying to swim
leave desire, whatever is past,
vanish into the unseen—
ah, that's what frightens her.

Leaving desire, releasing the past,
it's too much like dying.
Just thinking it frightens her.
Impossible to lie still.

She turns, sighs, a little like dying.
Closes her eyes—whatever waits,
easy, impossible, she can't lie still.
Night drops backwards, stark old cradle

closing the past. Whatever waits.
Unprotected, she's a newborn thing,
hushed, cradled, rocked back by night.
Sleep, it's like nothingness—

unprotected as a newborn thing.
How a child slips in, crosses that line:
nothing to it, sweep of breath,
rush of water—she's under.

ICE DREAMS

Backyard birds trill all year
about travel. They long for the chill
of high mountain reaches
they hear in migrants' song. Their lives
are easy, they know they've been lulled.
Eve imagines the Antarctic,
ultimate coast she never will see.

If soul lacks geography,
why does the thousand-mile curve
of one cold place wait
like a threshold? If she had nerve,
she'd be a long distance flier.
Off the horizon to a white night
of silence, magnetic extremes.

Slowly It Dawns

She wakes up light, a puff of cloud
    in a summer sky. Below her the city's
        rough diamond of glassy towers, faceted streets.

She wakes up blue, a splash of paint
    on a red canvas. Nude, missing one arm,
        her face zigzagging across pillow.

She wakes up with April blossoming in the room:
    if she picks fruit, she'll be punished.

She wakes up weary as if she searched all night
    barefoot over sharp gravel for that thing she lost,
        that piece of glitter, that bent dime.

She wakes up after nightmares about cleavers,
    cracked bones, taste of grass in her mouth.
        Her body feels four-legged, heavy with meat.

A gray dawn and birds streaming south
    like Earth is sinking.

She sleeps, she sleeps.
    The world changes in unthinkable ways.
        What she knows is a glimmer.

The Snake's Tutorial on Desire

It blooms like a burning bush,
howls like a dirt-yard dog.
Rises like a lark, falls like a kite.

Where does it come from?
Latin lovers: *de-sidere,* i.e., wicked little stars.
A bow & arrow & a naked boy.
The apple & the appetite, needle & spoon.

How long does it last?
Like a thorn-apple, sacred to Shiva
& fatal, it opens at night, closes by dawn.

Why does it change?
Thy neighbor's wife.
Brokeback Mountain.
The mistress of spices, emperor of lies.

Where does it end?
A dusty album by Dylan.
The trolley depot in New Orleans.

And what is the antidote?
The frying pan & the funeral pyre.
A candle, a high altar.
(Practice, practice.)

Radio Gods of the Low Country

On blue highways west of the sea she leaves palmetto behind for
pineland. Air changes, humid saltiness to panting heat.

Vacated shacks slump in wild tangles of green. Radio scan serves
up preachers: *God feels no pain. That's why Jesus had to be born.*

Beside the road, artemisia, scented herb named for a god, its common
name *wormwood*,
Hebrew for *bitter*. In Russian, *chernobyl*.

A stretch of nowhere, she might want a prayer but the second preacher
threatens.
Deny the Lamb of God and you'll suffer. Once *suffer* meant *allow:
suffer the little children to come unto Me.*

A town, where live oaks link limbs above the road and white-columned
brick repeats
surely as a homily. Old Victorians, verandas, beds of dreaming
hydrangeas.

Even NPR, some *Fresh Air*: famous surgeon who separates conjoined
twins says he sends them home with aspirin. *Babies don't feel
much pain. It's a learned thing.*

More false belief—she Googles it. The preacher said only God feels
no pain.
Sweet Jesus, what original sins we have.

Next, Buddhist monk. *We don't need God.* Nonattachment. *No
separation between us, just oneness.*

No god, surplus god. Everyone converts to the hallowed *lay me down
to sleep* habit.
She wants to lie down with *maybe*.
But she sings with the radio: *Don't mess with Mister In-Between.*

After the Burial

The Lord said to Cain, "Where is Abel your brother?"
—Genesis 4:9

Packing up Abel's robes Eve finds a torn photo
in a drawer. Blues are faded, reds like bloodroot
on animal skin. Feathery trees.
Boys with the beauty of gazelles.
They hold walking sticks as men would.
Wind lifts the innocence of their hair.

Behind them a trick of light flares
like a flaming angel—the way back blocked.

Years. How long they quarreled.
But here their eyes are blank coins.
Forever wide-eyed, halted on the brink.

Now the unendurable. She sent butcher-birds
for the murderous one then tried to call them back.
A swatch of scars marks days she knelt at the grave
of the gentle one and bled into his soil.

Oh, remember. What it was like to see them
head out on their own like orphans.

Adam, who never knew the word *parent,*
who thought up God and believed,
took Cain aside to mark him as his own.

Invocation for a Return Ticket

Let her not think of birds as returned spirits,
the recently dead humbled into plumage.

Small-boned, hot-hearted like that coal-dark
thing rasping in the sycamore, bitter
as a mother's grief. Not the gifted jay
who leaves a metal ring on the deck,
first anniversary after. Nor mourning dove
whose perfect feather falls at her feet.

Certainly not the little twits all hopped up
in the *Podocarpus*, nor, god help her,
veteran killers, the raptors. Not beauty queens,
swans and peacocks. Possibly flocking ones—
oh, souls of mass disasters—how suddenly they reel,
sky thrown into a feverish burst of ascension.

And the desperate phoebe, black-hooded,
strung out on nerves—teenager
who destroyed himself on railroad tracks.

But who knows otherwise?
She can imagine wanting flight after all this.
Song and warmth of feathers.

And How Does the Stubborn Stone Endure?

When drenched with rain it is stoic.
Sleet skips off its face, parched summers bake in.
        Windstorm, snowstorm, its contrary heart goes on.

Still, a little TNT or heavy pick, a sledgehammer,
some muscle—anything's innards can be knocked to bits.
        Just lose a lover, a child.

As broken chunks tumble, river waits.
Worn, ridden to ancient lowland, a new congregation.
        Their fine polish, each a tiny replica

of its ancestor. Down they slide. Ocean washes over,
throws back sand. Pale little smidgens. Fine silt of patience,
        wheeled off again to a deeper grind.

In the Therapist's Waiting Room

A week when floodwaters threaten
and news is catastrophic, she's still punctual.
Magazines are older, the room feels smaller.
She dreads that first moment, silence when she falters.
An untamable thing, the mind.
For days heart's been a crucifix too.
She could walk out of here and drive south.

To Baja, sit in the desert, its neutrality
of color. Then there's the blue gulf.
She'd rent a casita, learn to live with yucca and lizards.
Some say invisible stairs rise from the desert floor.
Every morning she'd climb. Past flutter
of *mariposa* is crow, then red flycatcher.
Every day, she could go higher.

In a Fiction

Should she have pitched her tent
in a place of ferns and fallen leaves?

What temptation would that have brought?
Easy to lose herself, no heart-to-hearts,

no recognition, no mirror as she grubbed
at roots, ate little, disappeared into a grove

of Balkan sycamores or den of dry moss.
Receding by degrees. Or easy to find herself.

But she settled in the city, married that man,
had children, studied trees, ate only their fruit:

figs, nuts, peaches, plums purple as a queen,
and combed her ferocious hair.

Untaught about heart, soft luxury
of honeyed songs, about scrabbling like a beggar

in love's dirt, how it swoops and clutches,
scavenges all it can, she could vanish,

alive only on the page, gone
to the silence of unimagined air.

FOUR

Vanishing Acts

You might wade in above the rapids,
tumble into a crevasse, pitch your tent
on a sinkhole, paddle too far out in the Pacific.

Sometimes it's not dramatic. You fall silent
at the dinner party. Tune out like a broken transistor.
Panic and go amnesiac during your big speech.
Take to your bed in a dark mood.

Perhaps your cell falls in the porta-potty
or GPS fails on the drive into the Mojave.

Tribes in the Amazon
believe dreams are the real existence.
To forget them is to disappear.

It's a great effort not to disappear.
Who among us can show up every day?

Even to enter this world is to vanish.
From the region of unblemished souls,
we all made a great escape.

His New Art

October, November, December
he lies awake at midnight unable to move an arm
to her side of the bed. It was a marriage
of brute disaster—first exile,
then murder, then her sudden vanishing.
Years together, now their big house
empty as a church on Monday.
He hires a cleaner, keeps the house
spotless as a man who never kept house can,
tries to remember her habits—
no clutter in the kitchen, but the cat
eats on the counter.

After work, he walks the hall,
discovers her absence again, starts to pick up
behind the dog, straighten kitchen chairs
already in their places.
March, he leaves the blinds open,
tries to let in light. Gloom
still hangs its stale banners. He takes a trip
in April, returns early—
misses that spectral solitude.
June, another round of weepy nights,
waking early, free-fall back.
Everything is still her.

He'll buy a new chair, a bright rug,
some piece of art.
Late August he finds a dark acrylic of a man,
his head cocked sideways to a night sky.
Takes down her oval mirror, hangs
his own reflected light.

Hejira

Sweetness in the air.
Wild anise and a flowering thing.
Wind scoops the trail's scent straight at her.
Now a rolling creature signals its fate.

Yesterday she watched five quail
flee into dense bush and flung rocks at them.
Four of the covey took flight, one lay
bleeding into dry leaves. She took it
in two hands and twisted its slender neck—
she didn't expect it to be so difficult
and the soft feathers agitated her. Ripped open
its chest with her own claws, lay this sacrifice
in fire. Then she grabbed it,
ate its burning flesh. How she smells now.

Always she imagines her daughters
behind her. They are running for it,
from their own disastrous lot. The red earrings,
pages of a book, everything she can spare
dropped along the trail. Today a blue kerchief
they'll recognize. She keeps dreaming
she's separated from a small child,
defenseless one, whose face changes
as it wanders off and her train speeds away.

Every day now, desperation. No point
to this path she thinks. But she goes on kicking up
dust, grabbing at berries, looking for a route
over the next eternal hill.

Refugees

One blind road then another—
our trek mapped a grim maze. Two days
we crouched in a chain of ancient caves

as icy squalls blew in. The instinct
for decency lives nowhere now.
The poor have no medicine

and streams disappear while money
flows upward. You try to read
the devil's message in callous bodies.

Our babies cry, food rots
then runs out. We flee to protect them
from careening bullets but learn

some wounds are crueler than others.
Keep to the rear, we were told. Safer there.
No. Sabotage aims for the last flank.

Scavenge with us. You'll find
sharpened points of forty battles,
evidence you're in this war too.

Ecclesiastes After Innocence

We thought we knew God but destroyed or lost Him.
Now we would do with the once-beloved
what we did with God.

If trapped in the garden again we would be innocent
as a late summer plum, heart forward,
all our holy thoughts of Him.

Under His law we were nothing.
When the once-beloved ruled us, we were nothing.
We could not live as nothing.

We were small and worshipful.
We imagined safety.
Now we feel small again, reliving the story.

Arrows of unhappiness strike us everywhere.
What we can bear and what we
feel shame for, the same.

The beast will rise again.
We cannot live with the beast
and the beast cannot live without us.

We would do with them what we did with God.
Let our snake-bit hearts be earthbound now.
A garden for worms and roses.

Sermon on the Mound

Each of us started in a garden,
communed with a snake.
Toads, libertines, prophets, damaged fathers,
bosses who favored us.
When primal fruits tempted us—
flesh of the apple, blood orange—
we bit. A hard fall broke our beliefs.

At our first communion we poured libations
to gods we hoped never to know.
Global keening, a chaos of tongues.
Unholy ones, forget innocence.
Count your sins like a nun on a chain
of cut beads. Either way, you feel
the florid claw at your heart.

But our wounds stir hallelujahs—
we would not have sought revival
in one another's arms without them.
Sisters, we've made rough beds together.

Sleeping in caves of feral mountains
on the cusp of winter. Shaking the pepper trees,
gathering juniper, chokecherry to spice the bloody quail
and skewered body of a sloe-eyed deer.

You who are scribes, invent new hieroglyphs.
Dip your feathers in strained beetroot,
use the beaten bark of a fig tree.
Once all poems were made like this.

Our runners will fly with them between camps
when moon begins its slide toward the south.

Will we survive here? The answer
whips through flames that exalt cities
into blackened psalms and toll the climax
of male trafficking. When curls of ravening smoke
recede, when the sky opens its blue heart—then.

Lilith's Psalms

Psalm of the Blue Ridges

Yea, we walk through wooded hollows where
we once courted love and meet only the animus
of male rifles. We fear.

Suffer blood of possum and secretive quail,
crash of the doe through doghobble.

We lie down beside the sweet laurel
amid toxic detritus of three-day partiers
who anoint themselves with firewater.

Our faith rests in mountain women picking banjos
who lead us from still waters to the two-step.
May the scent of calycanthus prepare us for slumber.

Mountain bikes crunch on gravel
and rampant machinery of builders rattles our ears.
Surely summer homes will overtake us.

We give thanks to ginseng and flame azalea,
autumn-hung hills that preserve us. The rusty
rod and staff of a trail sign. Yea, it comforts us.

And if we stray in yellow buckeye
or dense basswood, surely the lone ranger
and her green truck will arrive.

Psalm of the Four Corners

Alleluia with crow and bobcat.
Let anthems roll through the desert. For here
in the Great Basin there's solitude.

Once we ascended high places of Zion.
Yea, verily, now we look down
on Airstreams and concession stands.

Once Baptist Draw and Upper Chute Canyon
echoed in descant. Now engines of combustion
desecrate stone arches. Black Mesa
and the Kolob speak of larceny.

Make a joyful noise with tambor and hubcap,
sojourn in gullies of thrice-broken dreams.
Beseech backpackers to leave no scat,
pray new age shamans and ATVs run out of gas.

Blessed be deer and the antelope.
May ten-gallon hats of militant grazers
blow through the rabbit bush.

Silence of the rufous Escalante,
crusted spine of the Chuska
will lead us to deliverance.

And all the days of his life may Old Paint
ride around real slow. Amen.

Psalm of the Glass City

Walk through forests of glazed towers—
behold, no acreage below, only light-belted
buildings, high rise of suited workers.

Mountains tremble in their reflection,
clouds shiver across boardrooms—
how elegant the race toward dystopia.

Figs, almonds, and willows
grow on rooftops. Bee and bee-eater
nest in parapets.

Truly the poor were driven out
with the deer mice. Splinters of the past
rot under us and overhead,

only a blue limit. Shrill, the harbor's whistle,
clang-clang of silver.

Spotted cats, mink, fat-tailed fox ran
before trappers. Before sawmills, before miners,
carboniferous mosses slept in hillsides.

Before explorers. Before settlers or sightseers.

Who remembers native earth raising
red cedars? They alone scraped sky.

Psalm of the Traffic Stream

In the ceaseless onrush of I-80
clouds fly at us like soggy angels.
Stippled waters of the Bay murmur *lunacy*.

We thirst for the slow life yet hunger
for speed, turn our heart's gears at ten miles
over the limit.

Everyone has destinations.
Verily, we sing fascination with velocity,
of flirting deadlines and white-knuckling it.
Behold self-righteous ones who barrel
three lanes across rush hour.

Let us rejoice instead in upright travelers
and pray for deliverance from stench of big rigs,
adolescents who straddle the line while texting.

May we learn to be late for the appointment,
to be late for everything, not show up at all.
And blessed be the small voice
of indolent children we once were
who yearn for leafy solitudes.

Yea, how easy to drift, this road a cut artery,
the familiar one-way. Should a drunken motorist
demolish us, may we dwell among
rutted back roads forever.

FIVE

CAIN'S LAST SACRAMENT

He lunges into the school with a hooded
gun, delivers final rites to a girl reading a book.
Not a prayerbook and not the girl he meant.
He extracts penance from a boy wiping
lab tables and the bearded man crouched
behind a desk. Hail Marys for three harlots
streaking toward the exit. Red stigmata
track stairwells, spatter a cleaning woman.
Next floor: racing steps, door slamming,
then silence. Smell of fear, incense.
His bulletins stud bare wood, he hears
the missa solemnis of screaming. Choral moans
sanctify the building. Wheeling room to room
he has missives for the body, blood
for everyone. Then hot metal consumes him,
his looping brain blanks out, not the dark
angel he mimicked, but spaciousness,
mother who receives all, cleans holiness
from hearts, binds them. Communion.
No longer alone. With him, the rictus
of a boy's face, a girl's blinded eyes,
arms of a man reaching.

Since News Arrived

Outside, in the chill darkness.
Eve's made it her job to think about death.

Stars blink in fits and starts
as if she's to decode them. Maybe death

comes on that way: lit, pulsing.
Or like wind in the hedgerow

touching every needle, setting the cypress
in motion, but really nothing.

Since they gave her the news,
she's been here on the headland,

watching black waves. Slip away, surge.
Maybe it's a return. Maybe fluid.

Summertime, at night, by the sea,
it doesn't seem that frightening.

Back at the camp, women are mourning,
taking the infusion of other voices.

She's made it her job to think about death,
but, children, it's theirs to stay alive.

Lamentation for the Children

Children come, bringing bliss and wretchedness.

Come ready to be bruised.
Chaining us with soft tentacles of their openness.

Leave us pierced and threaded, bound forever
with thorns, singing behind the palings of love.
Like children. Though we are not.

Don't look back, not once, at the trembling
in your arms, the bed where they slept.

They return like pagans walking toward
mid-winter light. Flanks bloodied and broken
or fat, satisfied. Limbs scarred by the beast,
hearts blown apart or triumph in their throats.
Grown sharp or blessing us, decency in their faces.

We die for love of the children.
With each death uncountable more are born.

Always, the world's egg breaks open.

Acts of the Apostates

After the first one was assaulted
we lay beside the lagoon, washed her
with its brackish tears.

The second transgression, we raided
the weapons-house. We might bury them,
we might use them.

Two sisters were ambushed. We grew mute,
then spoke in tongues, sank into dreams
in the cold light of noon.

A mother raped, defiled. Her daughter
dug a grave for herself so only death could capture her.

Finally we all became love's traitors.
Like standing onshore to greet the tsunami.

Goats' bladders of blood,
hide pouches packed with gelignite. We sprint
by night, creep beneath barbed wire,
flee down fetid alleyways
as granite heroes fly off granite horses
like flocks of pebbled starlings.
Marbled columns of courthouses
collapse, veins cracked open.
Scarlet signatures everywhere
Slaughterhouse dross.

In remote wastelands or wilderness dugouts
we grow old. Night already presses down, a dark glove.
Remember how we hid at bedtime?

If the desert of our house is too silent at the end,
before we would go back
we'll unravel kindness from a rattler's tongue,
seek beauty in black and silver vultures.

Night Snake

Scaly wisp of creature
in the bedtime mirror, ruined
by love. Half babe, half reptile.
Darling, it's you.

No, me. Coiled up from the core.

A looking glass is a clear well—
an indecent pool where a serpent
lies. Look at those eyes—
keyholes of darkness speckled with light.

Just an animal, perishing like the rest of us.
Bloody little quail, the spike-horned deer
skinned after slaughter.

Latter Days

The back story was supposed to speak of love,
not tell an unbroken tale of siege and plunder.

Not of women trekking back to old shrines
for brief moments of ecstasy while children

slept beside junkyard dogs. We presumed music
from heirloom instruments, soloists hitting

mystic chords. Instead we got Incarnation.
Fleshly sacrifice. Praise for the goose and the shrew

on a collapsed altar. Layer by layer we dug:
rotting nooses, broken pews, cracked motherboards.

Wheels of large vehicles. A skeleton
with clasped hands, yoked fingers shattered.

No map, no threshold, no sweet chariot.
Nothing to tell us how far we are from home.

The endangered roam alien streets, a few days away
from starvation, open to snipers. We offer our poor

hospitality but they say no. Our safety is doubtful
and we too closely resemble the enemy.

Apologia for Exposed Roots

Give them beauty for ashes, The oil of joy for mourning.
—Isaiah 61:3

Forgive us, how we are ravished
      by the blossoming face of disasters.

We never meant to step outside and feel awe
      but after explosions killed forty strangers
sky bled a vein of jade and indigo.

The day a firestorm feasted on homes
      we felt a smack of reverence as noon sun
turned red and crippled gods appeared
      in the spiky architecture of blasted oaks.

Demiurge. Maker who buckled us
      to cataclysm, must want us to keep looking.
A land mine bares a filigree of exposed roots.
      A tsunami thumps open the sea's body like an egg.

Not to stand and gawk but see it all:
      and know it's about pain.

Forgive us. We need apertures, even a small fracture.
      Otherwise only a poor creature in the road—
animal, brakes, howling.

SIX

Also Light

Time, a short fuse.
Darkness winks around a corner
a mere handful of days since the Garden.

Mother of all, guilty acolyte, torchbearer,
peripatetic pilgrim, rookie guerilla.
The world warps fast, a poorly aged cradle.

But also light. Happiness—inexplicable—
coming in such a rush. Spring willows, devilish scent
of gardenias, skies bluer than a white wolf's eye.

Finally I'll unreel a day's pleasures,
settle into its sumptuous grip. Ecstasy
of daily routine: sunrise, moonset.

Winter days with scarlet feathers, chirred calls.
Backcountry like Eden, mountains
axed out by ancient ice.

Endless arrows zing inside where
I can't escape them. Hunger frets and growls.
But awake now, I can't bear to sleep.

Cherish dreaming so I can't bear to wake.
No longer given that life is fatal.

Revelations

Tell me how you fled and resisted until life
made you its minion. How you envy
animals who race for forest at daybreak.

How their coats speak of smoke and fire,
flicker with embers. How they howl
lunatic music of nightmares.

Remind me of sea-facing tamarind trees
and draw of bitter elm and salt sting
in a dry river's mouth.

Tell me how odds alter at the hour
of our birth. We'll tally our deceptions, risk this
and more when we meet.

Just find me before the Rapture.
Speak in a voice that comes and goes
like finches. If you must write, do it on my skin.

Notes and Gratitude

The first Eve poems came fifteen years ago but I never intended a narrative. Later I found myself writing dystopian poems, unsure where they were going. The flow of traumatized Middle East migrants filled headlines, the 2016 election unfolded, #BlackLivesMatter and #MeToo emerged. I better understood the wave I was riding. Raised in the South, family deeply bound to church, I grew up immersed in biblical and religious mythology. Years after freeing myself from its g-force, the beauty and structure of the Bible gave the book shape. Many contemporary poets also occupied me. Gratitude to these influences.

Thank you to Patricia Spears Jones for selecting this book for the John Ciardi Prize and giving it a public life. Her work has long been a vital voice in the community of poets. Deep appreciation to Jennifer Sweeney and Maggie Smith who gave the manuscript such careful readings. Their insights and suggestions improved it in uncountable ways. To my writing group, Thirteen Ways, endless gratitude: Robert Thomas, Idris Anderson, George Higgins, Melissa Stein, Zack Rogow, Jeanne Wagner, and Steven Winn. Brilliant poets and best readers! Special thanks to Robert and Idris who gave the manuscript its final readings and spotted all the places it needed polish.

Friends and family sustain me. Two dear friends in particular: Carol Jenkins, whose gorgeous art is the book's cover (see more of her work at www.caroljenkinsart.com), and photographer extraordinaire Ellie Waxman, who took the author photo. To my wife, Linda O'Brien, and daughter, Ana O'Brien Burch: you give my life heart.

Acknowledgments

These poems have been published in the following journals, sometimes in a slightly different version.

2 Bridges Review: "After the Burial" and "Radio Gods of the Low Country"

Canary: "Psalm of the Blue Ridges," "Psalm of the Four Corners," "Psalm of the Traffic Stream," and "Psalm of the Glass City"

Catamaran: "Apologia for Exposed Roots"

DMQ Review: "Vanishing Acts"

Elixir: "Ice Dreams"

Madison Review: "The Lilith Wind"

Many Mountains Moving: "October Noir"

Mudlark: "The Patriarch's Gift," "The Snake's Tutorial on Desire," and "Latter Days"

Salamander: "Invocation for Time/No Time"

Southern Poetry Review: "His New Art" and "In the Therapist's Waiting Room"

Split Rock Review: "Psalm of the Glass City"

Stoneboat: "Mother on Fire"

Tinderbox: "Since News Arrived"

Wherewithal: "At the Longest Red Light on Suburban Avenue"

Zone 3: "Invocation for a Return Ticket"

"Refugees" appeared in the anthology *A Very Angry Baby* (Acre Books) as "Asylum," and "Since News Arrived" was reprinted in the *Marin Poetry Center* anthology as "Since They Arrived."

Beverly Burch is also the author of the poetry collections *How a Mirage Works* (Sixteen Rivers Press), which was a finalist for the Audre Lorde Award, and *Sweet to Burn* (winner of the Gival Press Poetry Prize and a Lambda Literary Award). She is also the author of two nonfiction books on psychoanalytic theory and sexual orientation: *On Intimate Terms* (University of Illinois Press) and *Other Women* (Columbia University Press). An Atlanta native, she has lived most of her adult life in the Bay Area and has a psychotherapy practice in Berkeley, California.

Winners of the
John Ciardi Prize for Poetry:

The Resurrection Machine by Steve Gehrke,
                selected by Miller Williams

Kentucky Swami by Tim Skeen, selected by Michael Burns

Escape Artist by Terry Blackhawk, selected by Molly Peacock

Fence Line by Curtis Bauer, selected by Christopher Buckley

The Portable Famine by Rane Arroyo, selected by Robin Becker

Wayne's College of Beauty by David Swanger,
                selected by Colleen J. McElroy

Airs & Voices by Paula Bonnell, selected by Mark Jarman

Black Tupelo Country by Doug Ramspeck,
                selected by Leslie Adrienne Miller

Tongue of War by Tony Barnstone, selected by B. H. Fairchild

Mapmaking by Megan Harlan, selected by Sidney Wade

Secret Wounds by Richard Berlin, selected by Gary Young

Axis Mundi by Karen Holmberg, selected by Lorna Dee Cervantes

Beauty Mark by Suzanne Cleary, selected by Kevin Prufer

Border States by Jane Hoogestraat, selected by Luis J. Rodríguez

One Blackbird at a Time by Wendy Barker,
                selected by Alice Friman

The Red Hijab by Bonnie Bolling, selected by H. L. Hix

All That Held Us by Henrietta Goodman, selected by Kate Daniels

Sweet Herbaceous Miracle by Berwyn Moore,
                selected by Enid Shomer

Latter Days of Eve by Beverly Burch,
                selected by Patricia Spears Jones